The Dedalus Press

The Last Dreamers

Selected Poems

Pádraig J. Daly

Collections of Poetry by Pádraig J. Daly

Out by the Side of Things, Anthos Editions 1975
Nowhere But in Praise, Profile Press 1978
This Day's Importance, Raven Arts 1981
A Celibate Affair, Aquila 1984
Poems Selected and New, ed. Jack Harte, Dedalus 1988
Out of Silence, Dedalus 1993
The Voice of the Hare, Dedalus 1997
Dall'Orlo Marino del Mondo, tr. Margherita Guidacci,
                                    Libreria Editrice Vaticana 1981

The
Last
Dreamers

New & Selected Poems

Pádraig J. Daly

DEDALUS

1999

The Dedalus Press
24 The Heath
Cypress Downs
Dublin 6W
Ireland

for Michael and Róisín

ISBN 1 901233 45 6 (paper)
ISBN 1 901233 46 4 (bound)

The cover is from *Thebaide*: a 15th century painting by
Starnina. Uffizi, Florence
Dedalus Press books are represented and distributed in the
U.S.A. and Canada by **Dufour Editions Ltd.**, P.O. Box 7,
Chester Springs, Pennsylvania 19425
and in the UK by **Central Books**, 99 Wallis Road, London
E9 5LN

The Dedalus Press receives financial assistance from
An Chomhairle Ealaíon, The Arts Council, Ireland.

Printed in Dublin by Colour Books Ltd

CONTENTS

The Voice of the Hare

New Poems

Nowhere But In Praise

Na Prátaí Dubha

Dungarvan was a long and winding street
Of low whitewashed houses;
The Square was still a potato field
Full of the blackened fruit;
The hake was scarce, the fever ran everywhere.

In the countryside, bailiffs were emptying
The small houses;
They met little resistance.
The mountains would never be peopled again.
Whole hamlets were abandoned now forever.

Stones among nettles, a fuchsia hedge.
Mounds of fallen mud
Tell of the dead storying.
Some tried to grow crops on the reaghs
And fell by their unfinished ridges.

Mothers followed their children
In mock funerals;
There were processions at dawn
To the top of the road;
The burial place: America at the farthest turn.

Each day handcarts came through the town
To carry out the corpses.
Some were buried alive,
Taken up soundless from the roadway;
There was no energy for tears.

Until God gathered them
They would face back to the sea,
The fishing boats, the lines of thatch,
The smoke's silence, lights coming on in the evening:
All they ever knew of life or living.

They lay together in one grave,
Neighbour beside neighbour, husband by wife;
No poorhouse wall to cut man and woman
In two; or gates
To lock them from the countryside;

While their children, uncomprehending,
Cried themselves
To final sleep
And the dogs of the garrison
Waited for bones.

Family

Even in Winter,
With cold and empty skies overhead,
They rose with the light
And the earliest ebbtide
To feel for black mollusks
Along the sands.

I never heard them sing at their work
Or laugh and run wild
Like May potato pickers;
They moved purposefully among the rocks
In heavy greatcoats
Like huge primeval crustaceans.

They were not the happy poor.

Tertullian on Prayer

The birds of the air
Fly straight towards God
And spread their wings
In crucifixes;

The periwinkle
When he moves
First lifts an eye
To ask for strength;

The red cow
Coming from her stall
Looks up, moves forward,
Bellowing praise.

Final Letter to Elizabeth

I beg your forgiveness:
Why, I do not know
Except it be for my
Not having ever known
What to do or say
To befriend you;

For hesitating to reach,
And yet inculpable
Even in this
For if my wishes had hands
They never would have ceased
To comfort you.

And yet because I loved you once
And imagined love answer
In your slow eyes
And because love
Has foolish duties,

I write across the oceans
That separate us now
Begging forgiveness,
Putting my hand out
Lest either of us,
The time being near,
Should go out alone.

Sagart I

In many ways you're like an old man. Perhaps
You walk alone more than most people twice your age.
You notice each change of weather, the drift
Of smoke to sky. There is a certain decorum
You follow in your dress, the way you comb your hair.

You have many acquaintances, few friends;
Besides your unreplying God you have no confidant.
Nevertheless you lift your hat to all. Old ladies
Especially will seek you out, sometimes a sinner.
You are guest at many celebrations, a must at birth or death.

Sometimes you wonder whether this is how God intended it.

Sagart II

Every so often you withdraw,
Take twine, a dozen pegs,
And begin to mark off
A small exclusive corner
Of yourself.

But other peoples' cows
Come shoving against
Your walls and their chickens
Fall on your sprouting hedgerows;

And though you dig
Deep trenches all about
And festoon the place
With dangerflags,

People dumbly somehow
Stumble against it
And send you spinning
Farther and farther in along yourself
For peace.

Sagart III

Like old countrywomen
By fireplaces on Winter evenings,
We sit alone.

Outside day draws in; dogs
Bark to one another across acres
Of mountain; the last red hen
Goes wearily to shelter; younger
Voices rise and fall in laughter
Or argument; there is banging of churns
And milk poured quietly.

We have some urgent tale to tell
About life; but our mouths open
And no sound gathers shape.
We belong out by the side of things.

For Roses

Like last year's schoolchildren
You have drifted out of my life,
Leaving only the pain
And my unwarranted surprise
At your callousness.

You who were, through circumstance
Not will, moon and stars in my sky,
Rosegarden about my house,
Have made yourself
As the bright furze
On unreachable mountains

And yet what right have I
To sorrow? Nothing was ever written down.
We wound no strings of possession
About each other. No secret
Important words were spoken.

You owe me nothing beyond
The polite enquiry you sometimes make
Of friends who in their turn
Will drift and leave dark flowers of absence
For roses about my life.

Evening at Ostia

(In memory of Pier Paolo Pasolini)

When evening came, the red flowers were watered
On the balconies; the air was heavy with their scent.
The overflow dripped softly to the paving, like rainfall.
People came out now to walk in the coolness.

Tablecloths were spread outside the trattorie;
Under a stark white bulb, a man sold triangles of melon;
Microphones blared songs of tenderness from a circus tent;
Lions jumped, seals went through hoops, horses

Galloped on the sawdust. The wineshops were open
Well into dark. You could still smell the long flitches
Of the morning's bread. Someone argued far above;
Through a window, a new Caruso was singing.

There were notices forbidding people onto the pier.
Fishermen and lovers climbed, laughing,
Past the barriers; the sea itself
Was feverish and warm.

Cars sped by with their midnight revellers.
Brakes screeched at every crossing;
The crowds had gathered to where the light was,
The deckchairs were all folded, the sand raked clean.

So if he cried out, from this his last wilderness,
There was no one to hear.

Italian Journey

I don't remember even the name of the town:
The station was half a mile below
And we went upwards by a small stream
Green and stenching — like water in a vase.

It was morning. The schoolchildren
Wore smocks with bows intact.
There was a flock of geese barring our way;
A wellfed gander hissed his own importance.

We had an hour to wait for the bus
Which would take us farther into the mountains
To a fortress town someone knew
Where the women still used reaping hooks
And carried the sheaves home on their heads;
And it was too high for grapevines.

So we found a birreria with sunshades outside
And its doorway framing all the valley.
Someone began to name the distant villages:
Cave, Olevano, Genazzano, Guadagnolo.

And I spoke a poem in my mind:
Schoolchildren chased geese across it
And I could not tie the dancing sunlight
Down or the beer's frothing.

Vicar Street Flats

On Winter evenings
They stand, silent as mountains,
Against the sky

Until an unheard summoning
Brings the children
From door after door

Like the Hopi of legend,
Brought forth into light
Out of the belly of the world;

Or the people Signorelli saw,
With slow joy, tear themselves,
Limb after limb, from the earth.

They tie ropes round lamp-posts
And swing till nothing is solid
Or distant or fearful anymore.

Scene with Lights: Thomas Street

A darkening sky, six fellows with sticks
Can't manage to drive four black cows
Into Tyrell's Yard.

The skinheads outside the bookmaker's
Egg the animals on.

The lady in the fruitstall laughs
As the cows run towards the river.

A big car draws up;
A man gets out and buys bright oranges.

Immanuel, A Name Which Means . . . (Mt. 1,23)

He is the stray dog
Who brushes himself timidly against you in the street,
The city river that quietly climbs along the river wall,
Caressing in its loneliness the dull stone
And bringing dried-up weed to life;

The clouds when they lie in weariness over the earth.
The sun that touches them with black silver;
He is the rain flowing tenderly over the tar,
The leaves' excitement in the evening wind,
The frost like lichen on warehouse walls.

The world is a great sea
And he, the boat of varnished pine
That slips into the water at noon.

Problem

I understand Francis — all the stuff about the birds,
Throwing his clothes at his father, the singing, praising heart.

Once I travelled from Rome into Umbria
To his towns, his green mountains,
His fast streams,

Saw the coarse cloth he wore against cold,
The chapel shrining Chiara's hair.

Teresa Sanchez was never a problem:
In convent or covered wagon
In constant seesaw up and down towards God.

Or John
Soaring through his bars like a linnet in song.

But I am blind still to the Jew
My life traipses after;

And the spacelessness of God
Hesitates the hand I reach
Behind cross and tabernacle

Into his paltry loneliness.

Augustine : Letter to God

I

Where praise is impossible
I will praise;
And sing where sound faces silence.

I carry death about in me
And inevitable
Cold;

Yet I will sing
Or, failing,
Burst asunder with love.

II

Man cannot evade You :
Every wary mouse,
The ant that builds and climbs,

Each small limpet on a rock,
The waters sucked noisily
Through stones on the shore,

The sleek and watery cormorant
Compel him
To shout You out.

He is the phosphorous sea
Stirred to consciousness,
The cold gravels of the underbed.

From the acids of first time,
From the tepid waters of creation
He draws his voice;

And all creation —
Hills rising out of him
Into sudden seas,

Black shoreline,
The ocean's grit —
Binds him inescapably to praise.

And nowhere but in praise
Can quark or atom
Or any fraction else of mass

Find peace.

III

Each flower
Requires knowledge

And the raindrops
On the curlew's wing

Fall
As questions

There is a curiosity
In every piece of burnt wood.

IV

What am I
That You require me?

And what is my house
That You should come to it?

And what my love that
You demand my loving

And I am lost
Unless I reach and love?

V

I call:
And You are already in my voice.

I stretch:
And You are trembling at my fingertips.

You are here and smiling
While I send invitations out.

I draw circles to contain You,
Make clay jars:

But You are
Circle and jar

And the space within
And the space without

And the spacelessness
Without the final space,

Place
Where place has no meaning,

Time
Where all is an endless now.

I call
And I am my own answer;

I stretch
Only to where I have started.

This Day's Importance

John Street Hill

It happens only on days of bright sun
Or on clear evenings when lamplight
Breaks great corners out of the darkness:

The children are suddenly impelled
By the world of touch
We've covered over;

And with indeflectable purpose
Break open the watermains on the hill
Until high and glorious fountains rise into light.

They run back and forward
Beneath the spray
Like holy dervishes.

And all the sensuousness
Of buried clay and lively water
Fuels their defiance.

Dúthracar, a Maic Dé Bí

I need a certain comfort
For my prayer:
A house hidden in deep woodland
Near a clear stream
Where I can wash the dust of sin away;

I need birdsong too
And fertile soil to grow my crops;
And friends about the place
To set my heart to praise
The Mover of the Sun.

I must have bees
Above my head
And fresh eggs at morning,
Just enough covering
To keep the cold away

And give a certain comfort
For my prayer.

Fuar Anocht Magh Leathan Luirg

Fuit! Fuit!
The whole countryside
Is cold tonight,
The snow is higher than the mountains,
The deer can find no grass.

Fuit! Fuit!
Every stream is a racing river,
Every lake is a sea;
The horses cannot cross
The swollen waters.

No stone or hedge
Stands out from the land,
The badger and crane have gone,
Even the fish are cold
Under an icebound ocean.

No fledgling wren
Will last this Winter out,
The eagle's beak
Is frozen stiff,
The small insects are all dead.

We sit at our fire
Safe from the weather,
Pots purring,
Our feather blankets
Pulled about us.

Fuit!

Oisín to Patrick

I

Before you came with your God of shadows
And clattering bells, this hill
Was filled with light and trumpetsound :

Dogs barking at the chase,
The stream coursing noisily to the valley,
The women laughing as they gathered sloes,

Grouse and woodcock chattering in their dreams,
The foxes talking across the valleys,
The bittern lamenting the dark.

II

At evening we dug trenches in the ground,
Filled them with water to the brim,
Heated them with stones
Till they bubbled round our venison.

All Fionn's family came about,
The dogs stretched by the fires,
The young men at their song,
Cnú playing all bitterness away.

III

At Doire an Chairn where we stopped,
To match the beauty of its trees,
Fionn left loose a glorious singingbird,

Brought from blue Norway
And sweet enough to lure a saint
From the dead ringing of Christian bells.

IV

Fionn knew every sound of sea and forest,
The great boom of the tide,
The whistling of mountain waters,

The young deer pining through the night,
The boats floating against the sand,
The noise of bugle and hound.

At night he slept under the wide sky,
By river, stream
And thundering waterfall:

I never heard talk of bell
Or sorrowing psalm
Till now.

Lovesong

I can lay the scene out perfectly:
The river just where the trees begin,
Lamplight, stars, a little cloud,
A dark glow on the water.
I could have forgiven the world anything
But your sadness.

I can lay a second scene:
The hotel bedroom where you sent me to retrieve
A thing mislaid, still full of the scent of you;
The portiere's wife speaking suddenly
Through a box above my head, the white marble staircase,
Someone else's suitcases in the hallway.

I can remember too a day
You tried to creep upon the seabirds
And they fled when you came near.
Their underbodies, gleaming back at the sun,
The bright sea and yellow sands
Were poor counters to your loveliness.

I Will Miss You

I will miss you I do not doubt
Especially in the evenings
When the cicadas beat their wings
To compensate for the birdsong
The hunters have taken from our fields.

I will miss you when the firefly stirs
With a spark of the moon in his tail.

Bus-Stop

My bus is late in coming;
And you are waiting for me
Out where the fields begin.

Beside us, the newspaperman
Stuffs old posters
Into a plastic sack;

Near the corner of Via Romagna
A woman is lowering a basket
From her window;

A boy comes from the cafe
With ice-cream and lemon tea;
She begins to raise them carefully.

Under the shades two men take coffee,
A woman sits apart,
Wrists shackled in gold.

A waiter dusts crumbs efficiently
From the tables,
Wipes the counter clean.

Cars pass,
Sparrows gather at the edge of the tablespace,
There is a scent of bougainvillea.

I am sheltering from the sun
By the high wall of someone's garden,
Trying to understand

This day's importance.
My bus does not come:
You are waiting

Out where fields begin;
And you can watch sheep
From your window.

Magnificat for Catherine

Your mother's body
Softly glowing as alabaster,
You danced in her eyes.

Before ever you saw light
Or learned to scream
So lustily,

When you were totally unwashed,
I watched you
Move beneath her body,

Swimming in primeval fluid,
Sole inhabitant
Of your close and shadowy universe;

And when I reached out my hand
To touch you,
You kicked at me suddenly

Till like those mountain women
In our book,
I heard my words becoming song.

Tadhg Gaelach: The Birth

Into our world of rush light,
Of smoke and short Winter days,
Into our town of dried hake,
Cornstores, twisting lines of thatch,
Into all our darkness and sorrow,

Like a flight of dunlins
Landing on the waste of ebbtide,
Like a shoal of summer mackerel
Welcome through the water,
Like a highwayman suddenly
Upon the burghers through the trees,
His coming.

Like Autumn copper through forests,
Like fire across the heather,
Like a furnace blazing
Beneath her white body,
Breaking her apart with force of his love;

Walking where she walked,
Climbing where she climbed
(Lakes mirrorsilent in the Coums)
Slipping backwards
On the shaley hillsides.

And though the houses of the rich
Were barred against us
And the guns pointed from the windows
And the dancing never stopped
For the noise of our knocking,

The stable blazed brightly
At his appearing
And the whole world
Stirred with joy
Of his coming.

A Mháire, A Mhúirnín

I

The people have been coming to our house
Since evening,
The latch opening and shutting,
Footstep after footstep
Breaking the night silence.

Now there is no room anymore,
Your child is crying in a corner,
A woman from the town suckling it at her breast;
Soon they will be playing
The games of the dead.

I have no heart any longer
For their laughter or their tears;
I walk about the house
Like a man awake
In his most bitter dream.

II

What is happening in this house —
The noise of the people at the door,
You lying on boards,
Tuckers boastfully at your neck,
Your breasts wet still with mother's milk?

White cloth on your hair,
Dark cloth on the doorway,
Grey cloth on your shoulder;

Your lips fastened
And I cannot undo the lock!

What is happening in this house?
Why are there tallow candles
On the table?
Why is the air
Heavy with tobacco smoke?

Why are these people
Walking all about our floor?
Why did you ask them in,
Then leave me
To make them welcome?

Why don't you stand and walk
As you walked on Sundays
From the chapel?
Your head high above the crowd,
The people stopped to watch you passing!

III

Now that night gives way
To gradual day,
The cock crows,
The dew is lifting from the fields,

Old women are rising from their beds,
Young women are turning towards their children;
And the mother of my house
Is lying dead.

This is the time
For games to end:
There is no cause for laughter here
Only orphans wailing a dead mother.

IV

If death had need
To pass our town,
Why could he not take
An old woman past her time,

A mongrel dog
Or someone's cat,
A pet bird,
A pet lamb?

V

If you must go then and won't return,
Move through the people,
Whisper words of going:

Your father stands by the doorway,
Your mother is here in your house,
Your neighbours and children wait;

And I, who shared your bed,
Am stretching out my hands.

VI

Let us go off together,
Travel whatever roads you ask,
Call on friends and say farewells,
Through the mountains, past Clonmel,
To Ballyneill of the grey windows:

There I will leave you
And go to our children.

A Celibate Affair

Journey

Day after day
The caravans move through the hot sun
To the clay-walled city;

The walls rise suddenly where the desert ends,
Sharp shapes cut out of sun and shadow;

Animal after animal,
Huge relentless camels,
The children in light dresses running to keep pace.

These people have crossed treacherous passes and have lived;
They have followed rock-strewn roads
By steep cliff-faces.

They have lost animals to rain and thunderstorm
When the hard mountain floated like a torrent under them.

Here and there where grass is lushest
They make camp,
Sit at fires by night singing,
Prepare bread for their journey.

But always they must move;
And still they move;

If a man grows old among them
And the paths are steep and the ways impassible,
he will sit in some barren place
And sing himself calmly into death.

But always the caravans go onward;

Here at the gate there is laughter,
The women chatter,
There will be trading for flour and cloth;

They will salute old friends,
Exchange beads and trinkets;
A marriage will be celebrated into the long starry night-time.

But at the end, at every end,
They must go onward
As if ahead somewhere were destination;

And somewhere stillness.

Encounter

Monotony of sun
On sand and scrub,
A place of wild beasts
And long shadows;

At last he comes
To green and olivegroves,
Vineyards,
Houses climbing beyond walls
Along a hillside.

Here the tempter waits,
Full of candour,
Offering for easy sale
All the green kingdoms of the world.

And he,
Though gaunt from fasting,
needing rest,

Some perfect star
Seen a lifetime back
Determining him,

Passes slowly by.

Images

The wedding party has moved now
To a balcony over the sea;
The bridegroom is growing tired of photographs,
The bride adjusts her veil for the last time.

There are two boats on the ocean,
The sea is rippling over the hidden crown
Of a rock; elsewhere it is calm;
It is a warm night, Summer begins.

The clouds have become gold
And red and orange in the sinking sunlight;
They might background an epiphany of God.

I find no image here:
My mind walks on deserts still,
Empty spaces beyond the city
With stones thrown roughly about, jagged edged.

A man bent over rock, become rock.

Seamus Mac Cuarta: His Blindness

Under my feet
The grass of Summer swells abundantly;

And my heart stirs
For the singers who populate the trees.

I can smell the applebloom,
Wild rose, cliff anemone.

Only my eyes fail me :

Never will I watch the slow unfolding of leaves,
The quiet thriving of Summer,

Never travel blithely to the forest edge,
My mind set on
By my awaiting love.

Appointment for Dinner

We ordered cannelloni and a wine from the Romagna;
Suddenly it was night.
You threw a jumper across your shoulders.
Lightbulbs were shining in the vines above us.

We laughed more than usual;
You told the story of the fat man
Trying to mount a juggernaut
On the road to Ladispoli.

I remarked on the changes I had noticed;
You spoke of new apartments
Out on the Airport Road
Near where the Grey Donna used to live.

Night was folding in about us,
Vineleaves and lightbulbs cocooned us from the traffic;
Across the piazza shutters were closing.

We talked of inconsequential things.

At last you rose;
Nothing held you now.
We had passed each other by on the journey.

Elegy at Mornington

There are a few houses near the church,
Smoke comes from chimneys;

Here is quiet countryside,
Flat and undisturbed
Since the first voyagers.

Beyond the church
Old gravestones stand out against the sky.

Out there the estuary,
A causeway to the tide,
Vast mudspaces, seabirds;

A curlew is calling your name.

This morning the church was cold;
I knelt silently to remember you.

From nowhere
Gold light began to flood through windows,

Sparking the brass candlesticks,
Cutting the altarcloth in two,

Lighting the virgin in her niche,
Following the bright grains of the wood.

In its liberality
I make it your parable.

There is always something happening
Along the estuary:

Seeping of water,
Yellow flowers opening,
Birds descending in noisy flocks,

Appearing, disappearing,
Making figures of eight in the sky;

And youngsters always
Searching for something beautiful and strange.

You called your daughter Catherine,
Your happiness at her birth
A blazing, circling wheel of praise.

Nowadays she begins to walk;
She has taken over your smile,
Your sudden laughter;

And in this Summer light
I watch her clap her hands at songbirds
With your same wonder.

In the flat lands beyond your house
Swans call across the air,

The sands have covered over
The ruins of limestone castles.

Your house is sheltered by tall trees,
Your kitchen door opens onto meadows;
Horses in the distance race through yellow fields.

And nowadays your husband, for your sake,
Tends the desert of your garden
Into abundant fruitfulness.

Ballyvoneir

Long before life had cankered us,
I remember a perfect garden,
People who lived closely with earth and flowers;

An overhanging tree,
Lawns clipped to carpet smoothness,
Strawberries, smell of meadowland;

Two red setters striding with lean bodies
Through the high grass:
One returns holding a bird in his mouth;

An ivied doorway,
Noise of scissors,
Roses carefully gathered for a table,

Sun flooding through windows
Onto bright tablecloths,
The gleam of silver,

Long ago when there was hope
Before life had cankered us.

Among the Nettles

When we turn our backs to the sea,
It trembles still and climbs and falters;

On quiet hillsides families of foxes
Sport at evening
Where green pines slice the sun.

Glorious butterflies flit where no one watches,
Dun horses ramble by rivers and shake miraculous manes.

The willow grouse sits on her eggs all day
And holds her breath when danger comes
And stills at her will the beating of her heart.

In lakes far into the marshland
The grebe treads water in his courtship dance.

All day long the world is tumbling,
Stars follow their ordered ways,
Clouds form and reform.

A mind moves endlessly among the nettles
Full of the thrive of leaf and flower,

Hardly breathing or heaving,
Still as the willowgrouse.

Embarquement

You must walk over the mud
To reach the boat;

There are miles of emptiness to cross
Before you come to the channel
Where the river goes to sea.

Sometimes the mud is to your knees;
Seagulls will annoy you
With their hostile calling;

You must go over green slime
And keep your feet.

(If it rains, delay your journey).

You climb thick ropes to the hold,
The boat lists to its side.

Persevere!
In the evening
Great swelling of water will carry you.

After The Journey

The sea has turned silver,
The boats are cut in black on the water,
The rigging rings with the ebb of the tide;
At the end of the pier, a lighthouse beam is turning;

One immense cloud threatens us in the sky.

*

Perhaps the fables that sustain us
Are only fables;
And the God who breaks upon us
Like yellow willow breaking into catkins in April
While all the mightier trees are labouring towards leaf
Is someone unkindly.

Perhaps the love that lifts us
When hearts and bodies touch
Is a smoke of acids eating into wood.
Perhaps benignity is a dream we weave about ourselves,
Afraid to step out
Into the cold space of insignificance.

We cannot touch whatever lies beyond the tatterends of days;
Our longest time is moments long.

I am terrified that God will grow cold
And, after death,
Our minds hurtle forever through worlds of ice;

And the everlasting hammering
While the bird pecks at the stone.

*

Brendan sailed through islands of fruit
And barren islands
Until his boat at last reached the frozen sea.

For all of forty days the boat was stilled,
Their cries were all unheard.

At Easter they chopped the mast for wood
And, weeping over one another,
Lit their holy fire.

Came the thaw :
Morning dawned on sungilded sea,
Bright islands appeared again on their horizon.

Once a crystal mountain drifted by them :
They heard hopeless wailing.

A man hung on the ice,
Living out his death alive.

*

Cataracts of blue speedwell
Falling from the fences onto the fields,
Blackthorn coming into flower
Before coming into leaf,
A pigeon's flight linking tree to tree :
Here is manageable space.

It is when we look beyond
And the mind rolls towards stars
That we must turn fearful
And wonder how we presume
The world is plunged in goodness.

*

Suddenly
As when a child darts
Towards some wonderful butterfly
By the cliff,
We dart;

And there is no angel any longer
To guard us from tumbling out forever.

*

Once they took me into the country;

The hedges were full of Summer,
We climbed high fences to cross the fields.

At last I climbed the highest fence of all
And dared not jump.

A man came back for me
With candid eyes.

When I was midair he turned,
Ran laughing into the spinning green.

*

A bird flies through day perpetual
Like a swallow bringing clay to the eaves in early Summer.

He pecks at a brass pawnshop ball
As big as all the world.

As each million years goes by, he pecks,
Million after million.

And when that ball at last is disappeared,
It is the first day of all the world.

*

The settled lines run out :
We cannot by thought prove love
Nor is there science to reason us to trust.

Yet in silence
A certainty
Like a lone bird appearing out of white distance
Takes shape,

Something as strong and definite as a tree
Or a rosebush pushing a thorned branch out of the earth
Or a blackbird or a river or a star;

Or in the dust of cities,
A laburnum,
Grown tall and stalky in its climb to light,
Shaking liquid branches in the fabulous sun.

Poems Selected and New

Prisoner

A door closes behind me
And another door
And another;
Keys rattle.

There is no hope here but to wait,
Nothing to be expected.
We grow round like battery fowl,
Attack one another.

Nights are long;
At dawn seagulls flock beneath our windows
For feasts of excrement.
I wake each day to their shrieking.

Dinner:
Someone stares through my peephole
While I chew;
It is a world of eyes.

In the afternoon
We circle small spaces for exercise:
My mind circles its small space endlessly.

Some grow quiet as days go by,
Slip into madness
As shipwrecked souls from hopeless lifeboats
Slip with small splashes
Into sea.

Some explode suddenly,
Lighting the sky
Like Catherine Wheels,
Spluttering to futility.

I am become expert in the trivia of creation:
The grass in cracks,
Groundsel pushing stubbornly through tarmacadam;
Hawksbeard and dandelion stun me with their persistence.

Today my books were removed while I was out
As if they were guns or swords.

We are paradigms of some enormous failure.

Can your wives comfort you in your comfort
While we languish,
Close your ears to the banging of doors,
Our unmanning?

Guard

Once you go under the arch,
It is as if you were never elsewhere;
And the world of sparkling lawns,
Children cracking open eggs,
Squabbling through the half-sleep of breakfast-time,
Never existed.

You take on sin with your uniform;
And you float away from love
Like a legendary swimmer caught in currents
That drag him to a dismal underworld
Where life is lived in caverns
And bats spring eerily out of shadows.

And if you try to reach out,
Something constrains your stretching arms;
And you have no voice for voicing tenderness.

The greatest danger comes
When you carry your underworld back out;
And the brightness of grass
And flowers and eggs
And your own children laughing
No longer touches you.

From A Vietnamese Takeaway

The Irish?
They come after midnight
To empty their bladders against our van;
My sister trembles when they approach.

They take food at our counter,
Then refuse to pay,
Vowing to burn us out if we insist.

They call us "Chinks" as if we were Chinamen —
And tell us we boil gulls in our curries.
For sport, they shake the van on its wheels,
Laughing uproariously at my sister's screams.

Sometimes stones clatter on the roof.
Once men in balaclavas came with guns.

Next year we will be in a new place.
We will take memories with us of the Irish.

Out of Silence

Errand

Carrying his knapsack,
He shuffled out in his boots
To where the stars hung burning.

The winds of space assailed him.
He was a speck
Smaller than a sootflake.

Dejected by vastness,
He wrapped himself in himself,
Hugging his own warmth;

Till the immense God,
Waking from his dream,
Brushed time and distances aside.

Genesis

I

In those days God walked arm in arm with him in the garden.
Light breezes stirred the apples as evening fell.
One by one the birds gathered to receive names:
The fractious sparrow it was who convinced him of loneliness.

II

Thinking they dreamed still,
They awoke deliciously to one another;
High above, the skylark was a speck of song in the sky.

III

The first time he saw Autumn in the trees, he wept;
The glow of decay had never entered the garden.
he made a bouquet of red leaves for her,
More to his heart than all the garden flowers.

IV

Two pheasants rose from the bushes
As if disturbed in a conspiracy;
Then everything was hushed;
Rounding the hill he came upon the sun
          rippling on a great water.

Thomas Merton

What is to be said about silence
Except that it is;
And you sought it out diligently in your woods,
Living alone with your books,
In the company of birds;

Walking to morning prayer on a snow carpet,
Nothing there before you
But the marks of the monastery cat
On the white ground;

Or the form where deer slept
Close to your window,
Rhythmically heaving with your sleep's heaving?

And there is little you can send us out of your silence
Except to say that it is;
And it cries out louder than our clamour.

Duvet

Knowing my love of comfort, warmth and sleep,
Some friends gave me a great feathery eiderdown
To ease my Winters.

It will take me like Sinbad
Into lands of strange giants and peoples.

I will unfurl it to the wind
And sail like Brendan round half the world.

I will make a cloak of it like Bodach an Chóta Lachtna;
And when I stretch my arms
Kingfishers, wrens and tiny birds of every colour
Will whoosh from under it.

I will make a tent of it,
Stretched on poles as Yahweh stretched the sky.

It will be my sunshade near warm tides,
My bivouac in lands of snow.

I will spread it on the ground like the Roman widow
And build my basilica on top.

I will put it down on swamps
And build a bridge.

I will line my hollow walls with it
And insulate my ceiling.

It will be my meadow of Summer flowers
In dark December,
My noisy cataract, my Comeragh lake.

May the Lord prosper those who gave it,
Fill their mouths with music,
Bathe their bodies in buttermilk.

May their sheep lamb twice each year,
Their hens lay double eggs,
Their cows flood Ballyclough with cream.

It will teach me to think kindly on human hearts;
And on the heart of God
Who covers us always with undeserved kindness.

Prelude

God was in heaven then,
Bearded,
Smelling of sweet porter,

Surrounded by angels;
And everyone we could think of
Who had died.

When thunder rolled,
We knew the dead were knocking hurdles over;
And boisterous angels fell from horses
At heavenly Point-to-Points.

From a window over Rome
A man with silver spectacles
Dispensed infallible truth.

There was forgiveness for the bad;
And suffering was good,
Nobly borne.

Then God saw all that He had made
And found us
Comfortable.

Pentimento

I

He created emptiness first;
Then threw the world out like wool
To dangle amid the planets.

From the wet earth
He drew animals, bats,
Fish and coloured birds.

To one only
He gave a mind to range the stars;
But bound by clay and death and foolishness.

Sitting back, he laughed;
While men and women
Built draughty palaces.

II

Beyond the far reaches of the heavens
He is gone;

Beyond the last planet and star,
Where everything is wind and dust.

We cry out;
But if he hears,
He moves away from our voices.

III

He returns once more from the hunt,
With dead wildfowl braced across his shoulders,
Whistling as he goes.

A lone greyhound precedes him,
Scenting us out,
Warning him of our approach.

Thérèse

At one corner of the courtyard they grew nettles,
Lush and cruel as the giants of their most fretful sleep.
The older women took them to their beds
in pious atonement of sin.

Thérèse had penance enough in broken waterjugs,
A nun clicking her teeth as she prayed,
All the agony of constant closeness;

And in her room at night,
She shivered at the thought of God growing strange
And a death as final as the death of stars.

Believer

Lured by a light
Discerned distantly,
He trekked across the rolling ocean.

It might have been
The random glitter of a fish
That drew him;

Phosphorescence of plankton;
Or a far planet
Reflected on the water.

The seas grew rough
As he travelled;
Sky and ocean together turned grey;

But he kept faith still
With that single silver gleam.

June 1943 : Pause at Ötzal

We were in a valley between two peaks;
Snow glittered on the high wastes.

In the fields women were piking hay onto poles,
Trees were giant keepers of stillness.

Gentle Austrian voices spoke along the platform,
Another train shunted near;
People crossed to our empty carriages.

Soughing softly we moved again :
An old man near me murmured a psalm.

Never before was murder so innocently done.

Apocalyptic

I

First of all it was the sheep dotted along the hillside :
They began to give birth to lambs without legs.

Then, nearer the town, cows yielded dangerous milk;
Calves were stillborn or slithered out with two heads.

We were told to keep indoors,
To avoid eating rootcrops and drink only bottled waters.

Several unusual illnesses have been reported :
The old are especially vulnerable.

We are assured however that there is no cause for alarm;
The government is vigilant, everything is under control.

This morning little Vivienne died :
She was her father's joy,
She used to play on our roadway and sing.

II

We are late and long
Crossing this unfriendly city,

Walking on boards above the mud,
Climbing mounds of rubble.

Everywhere there are huddles of people around fires;
Grey ash blowing, suffocating smoke.

We have found no one to save us in this place;
The inhabitants are dour and bittertongued.

Fish swim to sea in combat suits
And dogs are born with mackerel heads.

III

What use the rolling in and out of the sea,
Caressing into form the ruin of the world?

The buildings will all be sand.
The roadways we have blasted hills to make
Will fall into the valleys;

The gardens terraced above the water,
The scented woods.

And there will be no one to watch the orange ball of the moon
Hanging above the white tide.

Intruder

You came from that early time
Before I began to lay my garden out
With its lawns and rockeries and wroughtiron chairs;
Plots of thyme, lupin, marigold,
Broom grown from seed
Gathered one Autumn on a slope in Lazio.

Meditative swans glided among the lilies,
Peacocks, like dandies, strode the lawn,
The country birds made nests in the hedges.
I planted nettles, too, to draw coloured butterflies
And purple stock to scent the twilight air.

I had happily banished you and all the time of your cruelty,
When you came, full of smiles,
As if we had been together days before,
Trampling as you walked
All my glorious borders.

Remembering My Father

I

When they thinned the woods,
Dormant bluebells sprang up everywhere;

This Summer, four perfect lilies
Came suddenly in the garden
Where no one had planted them;

In the grass beneath my window
Some small invisible thing beats insistent wings;

Your silence is full of signals.

II

Going to see you in Cork was the worst,
Your memory gone, your light faded.

The ward was in the dungeon of the hospital,
The chairs fitting tightly by the beds
So everyone could hear when we talked.

The doctors were always absent;
The nurses humoured you like an imbecile child.

How could I explain to them
That you shone like the Daystar once?
We basked like fat fishes in your brilliance.

III

No matter how much you walked at the end,
Your lungs were thwarted by the flowering cancers.

When I recalled tales from your past,
You begged me to write them down

So you could hold them like rails to lift yourself again.

IV

Four weeks before you died,
You wanted to see the graves in Ring.

I had forgotten where they were;
But you, whose memory was gone for recent things,
Walked me to them across the uneven ground.

Later, near Kenneally's,
You spoke Na Prátaí Dubha word for word.

I wept as you recalled the breaking up of a world;
But for a closer breaking.

V

We can see Leagh from the churchyard
And the gaudy cornfields of Gortnadiha.

The tide is full in the Bay,
Boats sail by the Cunnigar.

You could never comprehend our need to be elsewhere
With all this blossoming world about us.

Geese sit on the sea,
Dunlins move in gusts along the shore,
Water laps against stone;

Your silence is full of signals.

Leagh

for Senator John Daley

They were on that hill
And scattered round its hollows forever,
Making land of land at the last edge of land.

What happened us to abandon their fields,
Fleeing to towns and terraces,
Sailing to cities never heard of on the mountain?

Soon no one will remember their laughter,
The farmyard clatter, the cursing after dogs,
Milk spilling clamorously into churns;

Floury spuds emptied from pot to table,
Cream poured plentifully, chimney bacon,
Thick wedges of bastible bread.

The sleek greyhounds,
The marvellous horses that raced the fields,
The tall spectacular foals
Are all no more.

Ó Rathaille : The Dead Priest

The fragrant apple rots,
The tall tree, the blossoming branch,
The palm of Paradise;

The harp God's fingers plucked,
The psalm singer,
The gentle tongue.

Mercury is dead;
A blazing torchlight none might quench,
A hound for speed, an ox for strength.

Mary's servant is dead,
her bodyguard, her weapon;
Huntsman and wound healer.

Philosopher clever as Solomon,
Ship's captain,
Peacemaker, generous giver.

The very air now is heavy with grief,
Rivers flow onto fertile fields,
The sun is shedding tears.

London, April 1988

I

The tiny gardens of London
With their rhubarb clumps,
Misshapen appletrees
And brave clusters of daffodil
Are full of loneliness
That were full of you.

We need these little spaces;
And then the wide space of eternity.

II

On the train today
A girl in white sat opposite
And never spoke;

We pass one another by in the city,
Never stopping, never speaking,
So many of us,
How will places be found for us in paradise?

III

Outside the church, a Limerickman, down on his luck,
Wonders whether he might trouble me for a pound.

Inside, the baptismal pool
Drowns the dull hum of the street in waternoises.

The apse is lit by coloured saints, ⌒
The altar is a large square of gleaming linen.
I can smell freesia and roses.

At the Offertory they carry your prayerbook forward,
Your uniform, a green plant you tended.

Your coffin stretches before me as I lead the prayer.
Break the bread. am broken.

Milan

First there was a brown wall crumbling along by the roadway;
Then a field of ripe wheat with towering heads of thistle,
Red poppyflower.

Then a park with footballers;
And pigeons making commotion in the trees;
High apartment blocks, flowerstalls, dusty streets;

And all the people of the city
Hurrying past with urgent purpose,

Each held to each by webs of importance;
Such as save us
From plunging beneath the great wheels of buses.

The Voice of the Hare

He

He is somewhere in the garden,
Kicking up the leaves with his feet.

Nothing disturbs him.

He does not care any longer
Whether we eat the fruit or no.

Complaint

I will tell you, Sir, about a woman of yours,
Who suddenly had all her trust removed
And turned to the wall and died.

I remember how she would sing of your love,
Rejoice in your tiniest favour;
The scented jonquils,

The flowering currant bush,
The wet clay
Spoke to her unerringly of benevolence.

I remind you, Sir, of how, brought low,
She cowered like a tinker's dog,
Her hope gone, her skin loose around her bones.

Where were you, Sir, when she called out to you?
And where was the love that height nor depth
Nor any mortal thing can overcome?

Does it please you, Sir, that your people's voice
Is the voice of the hare torn between the hounds?

Sorrow

I am eating, drinking, sleeping, dreaming sorrow.
Yesterday I followed a small child to its grave;
Today, an old man.

I watch one I have grown to love,
Beautiful as the wind, languish;
And I flounder in the grief around her.

I sit with husbands in little smoky visiting rooms,
Parsing your reasons;
With broken mothers, with dismayed children.

Your people mutter bitterly against you;
How can I carry them?

Ministers

It is we who are kicked for your failures;

When pain lasts across the night,
When people gather helplessly around a bed,
When grief exhausts the heart,
It is we who must bear the anger.

When love fails,
When friends are gone,
When worlds are rubble,
When eyes cannot lift to see the sun,
People ask us to explain; and we are dumb.

When rage against you is a fierce sea
We are the first rocks on the shore.

The Last Dreamers

We began in bright certainty :
Your will was a master plan
Lying open before us.

Sunlight blessed us,
Fields of birds sang for us,
Rainfall was your kindness tangible.

But our dream was flawed;
And we hold it now,
Not in ecstasy but in dogged loyalty,

Waving our tattered flags after the war,
Helping the wounded across the desert.

Margaret Porete

On the fourteenth day, I came to the beguinage;
My rooms were simple and silent.

Outside, the fallen leaves were intensely yellow
As if they held in themselves the secret of light.

From my door I watched the sensuous flow
Of rain along the rooftops;

The pathways were covered afterwards
With limpid waterpools.

I was aware of the Godness of God,
His difference and his nearness.

And, even as my heart was ravished,
I became conscious of enormous evil,
Waiting with book and virtue to undo me.

*(Note: Margaret Porete was a Beguine Mystic who was put to death by
the Inquisition in Paris in 1310)*

Bill

a friend who took his own life

He did not hear the birds sing this morning,
Nor the waters whisper along the dykes.

He did not notice how splendidly the rising sun
Was recreating the sheepcovered hill.

He could not think of the small boy,
The wife, the girls he left sleeping.

In a world of light
He trekked a deep tormented darkness.

In the middle of love
No love could reach him.

On a broad mountain
He walked a dark tunnel,

Untouched by spring, untouched by hope,
From which there was no exiting.

Place of Death

I

It tears me apart to leave you,
In all your ravaged loveliness,
In this duplicitous place.

I recoil from the suffocating concern,
The drugs destroying inhibitions and logic,
The carpets and primrose rooms.

I cry against the plausible tongues
Cajoling emaciated bones into frilly nightshifts;
The trivialisers of sorrow, painting gaudy colours on worn faces,
Camouflaging falling tufts with silly bows.

How can we be at home
With people who converse daily with death
And are sane?

II

Here where people wait to die,
Someone has planted hopeful daffodils;
Tulips cluster boisterously at the doorway.

But the people who walk by us
Have purple daubs on their faces;

And upstairs in her room,
Elizabeth, who vowed to taste death neat,
Asks for morphine, begins to titter.

The Prayer

in memory of Margherita Guidacci

I

The rain was the heaviest I ever remember in the city:
The bus ran constantly into floods.

At Piazza Monte Sacro
I bought an umbrella and roses.

You were with friends,
Examining a photograph,
Snapped some Summer of your childhood.

You had lingered with the adults
To talk to an old countrywoman coming from the fields,
Your lively face eating the moment full.

Today you are a child again;
Your speech is slurred,
You cannot move without help.

You ask me to pray for your death.

II

If I were set down again on the street
Where we met after years of letters,

I would know it by the great stones of the Roman wall
That darkened it;

And the rush of steps
Leading to a dilapidated palazzo.

We lunched in a restaurant nearby,
Sitting indoors out of the heat.

I remember a fridge purring beside us,
Arches between the rooms,
Blue murals of Naples.

Our talk coursed down a thousand laneways,
Each of us needing to speak and hear at once.

When we looked into the street again,
Night had fallen.

III

A friend telephoned with the news of your death;
It was a grey June afternoon.

I put the receiver down
And thought of rain, roses,
A room with high ceilings,

You shrunken as a fledgling bird;
The prayer you begged for and I could not make.

The Weary God

He drives his pale flocks
Along the untarred roads
That lead into the hills.

Attentive only
To the noise of their bleating,

The tick of insects,
Ululation of wildfowl;

He has no heart any longer
For the anguish of the streets.

God

All day long
She has been arranging our welcome :

Scouring down the house,
Sweeping under beds,
Pulling out the old crocheted counterpanes,
Shining glasses and tableware,
Dusting sideboards and pictureframes.

Now she sits in a deep chair
Till we come crunching under the beeches
To the door.

Prayer

We gather at the river's edge;
One by one in the darkness
We place our flames on the water.

We watch them drift,
Fragile, flickering,
Out to the unsleeping ocean.

We fear at first that they will sink;
But the water carries them past every hazard
As if it loved them.

Divine Fox

The fox comes close to the house
On sunlit mornings of Summer
Before the ladies of the convent finish prayer.

He is secure in his own beauty,
His coat standing out dazzlingly from the grass.

He does not linger;
When he sees us staring, he disappears.

He is there also in Winter
When darkness covers the earth;
And everywhere.

A Thought from Tauler (Sermon 37)

Set the butterflies free,
Let the birds follow, out from their cages;
And the small exuberant pups.

Before you go into your house,
Empty yourself of all thought,
All shapes, all imaginings.

Be at home in spareness and peace;
See how He will come,
Ransacking your rooms,

Tossing everything this way and that
Like one who has lost a treasure;
opening doors and wardrobes,

Searching under chairs,
Behind cushions,
Emptying drawers onto the floor,

Until He finds you.

Relatives

Some of them knew little English
But spoke the old tongue
With the ease of skaters ranging over ice,
Of acrobats floating on the empty air.

Their words haunt my words
And I carry the ghosts of their sentences in my head
Like an unshareable secret,
Like a hunted faith,

Like a song I must sing,
Like a lovepoem,
Like a lament.

Uncle

I never remember him joyful,
His tall figure bending over us,
Talking only of ailment;

Or sitting at the fire in the dark kitchen
While the sun was poured like grace
On the mountain.

There were tales we heard of how powerfully once he played the
box,
How dexterously he could plait a rope,
How deftly train a dog.

But week after week we never saw joy :
Only silence and pain;
And heavy worry on our father's face.

We grew up under his shadow,
Learning early
How precarious is the human hold on happiness.

Minnie

I

After all the feuds and squabbles,
The quarrels about trespassing cattle,
The imagined slights,
The carefully hoarded grudges,
The pain (whatever caused it)
That made you build walls of aggression around you,

Like a boat, serenely, on a sea after storm,
When the sun newly lights the waters,
You lie in your hospital bed,
Grateful to the nurses,
Reaching to grasp our hands,
Slipping gently into God.

II

You put the memories of your oldest brother aside
And the other you had stayed by
Through years of unrelenting depression;

You blocked out the poverty of your childhood,
The mother cherishing secret griefs,
The gentle father favouring your beautiful sister over you.

You constructed a world that should have been;
Where your family shone above others
For the plenty on its table,

The warmth round its hearth,
The brilliance of its children,
The profusion of thrushes in its hedges.

You made isolation a blessing,
Observing every stir the insects made,
Listening to the night-soft muttering of birds,

The hushed tinkle of heatherbells.
You exulted in the hurts you inflicted,
Preserving yourself from the insecurity of affection.

At the end you refused to take food,
Hurrying to die,
Believing that beyond all our tawdry living

Unbearable happiness waited.
There were roads in the past that might have led elsewhere :
A farmer in the Comeraghs you would not be matched with,

A Canadian airman during the war,
Jobs up the county that never lasted.
So I weep,

Overcome by grief and love,
For the life you had
And all the lives that might have been.

III

You never let us swot a fly,
But made us shoo them gently out of doors;
You cupped your hands around spiders and lifted them
To where they might more blithely string their webs;

117

You captured wasps in a glass,
Releasing them gently onto flowers;
You taught us to attend to bees in overhanging branches,
To grasshoppers in the windless meadows.

It was no surprise then
That when we gathered for your funeral
A guard of butterflies waited in Seanaphobal chapel;
They fluttered round your coffin,

They landed on forms and windows,
Even on the altarcloth;
They came to offer homage,
You sent them to us as proofs.

IV

Your death was like a healing,
You went so happily into God.
Old friends came for the funeral,

People you had hurt spoke kindly of you
As if whatever caused your rage
Was dead with you;

And we could see in our minds
The little girl who gathered whorts
Till she was black and late for school.

Housekeeper

They grew old gradually together;
She was as close to him
As any woman is to any man,

Cooking for him, making beds,
Handing out keys,
Fixing funeral times.

In the evening each one sat alone :
Praying, reading,
Watching news and sport.

They kept separate rooms;
But all night long
She heard his every cough,

Every turn he made in sleep;
Yet she may not rant before his coffin
Or dress in mourning clothes.

Year's Ending

The crows gather to repossess the woods,
The river follows its silvery way,
The mountains begin to slip into darkness.

Soon only the sky will be real
And the houses pressed like tinsel stars
Onto the rim of the hill.

New Poems

Prayer in the City

In a room high over the city,
The old man knelt.

He asked God to bless his walk,
To carry his prayer up endless steps,

To defend his bones against cold,
His mind against forgetfulness.

He prayed for all who travelled below,
For all who were sick or in pain,

For all who were dead;
His heart flooding with love

For the great beings of creation,
The tiniest objects of the universe.

Feather

A white feather
Floats past blackened bricks
Onto the ground below.

I retrieve it
To remind me of a sunlit day :
The silence near at hand,

The noise of traffic from the street,
The calls of dealers offering fruit
And cut price lemonade;

Greying granite,
Blue boarded windows,
Green lichen on a chimney stack.

On her high perch
The preening pigeon readies herself,
Spreads her wings,

Then drops through air
As if flight
Were an ordinary thing.

Presence

If God is anywhere,
He is rapturously here, early at morning,
In the grey of an English Council Estate :

The skies hold back the rain,
Bins stand in squat order,
Buses move gravely from stop to stop,

Cats forage on a green
Littered with bottles and empty cans,
Crows quarrel for the remains of battered fish;

Doors open,
Faces emerge
To the icy touch of day.

A Presbyterian and Christ
(After the Scots Gaelic of Anna Mic Ealair)

You drew close to me
Beneath the juniper,
Became my companion
In the apple orchard.

Your closeness is sweeter
Than the finest wine;
When you gave me your love,
My body melted.

You gave me your love,
My body melted;
And I was forced to say :
"Hold back your hand".

Bridie Murphy's God

I knew him in bright shadows behind the cowhouse,
Where dung was piled
In fragrant heaps;

In fields where white geese foraged,
In the dark places of the hedgerows,
In pasture and copse,

In all the nests of eggs —
Crows' nests in high trees,
Thrushes' nests in the bushes,

Nests of truant hens,
Nests after mowing, full of screeching scalds,
Nests in uncut fields.

His scent overcame me in the dying grass :
I could not bear his closeness.

Comfort

I have been comforting your people
But their agony is so great,

Their need so clamourous
(And I am so empty)

That I have come back
To ask you to tend them yourself.

Ministry

She was lying amid flowers,
Sunlight erupting through the blinds behind her.

Seabirds called.
There was crying from another room.

People were asking me why.

Bartimaeus

I call out as you go by,
Insisting, like him, on pity,
Insisting on relief from an all-suffusing pain,

My body begging to be blessed,
To be touched,
To be comforted;

And you pass,
Not looking, not reaching to help me
Lift myself from myself;

At night, I lie down weeping;
At daybreak, I wake
To the heat of my tears.

Fugitive

Maybe I could find a life in Rotterdam,
Where love is cheaply bought
And comfort is commodity;

Or in Sorrento,
Wintering over a shut shop,
Watching paint lose the battle with salt and gale.

Or I might flee to Geneva,
Where people live privately beneath mountains,
Cold and unbeloved as this heart.

Ward

Some of them have been here for years,
Carried from bed to bath,
Envious of those
Who move like snails on frames
Or manipulate chairs with fingertips.

What is the great picture
That comforts you, Lord,
When you look at them?

Three Movements in a Mourning

I

I found your part of the beach today,
Crossing the rocks to escape the crowd;
The sun was setting the wet shingle alight,
Gulls called,
Sanderlings teased the tide.

The world followed its affairs
As if your being,
Young then
And shaking golden hair,
Were of no consequence.

II

And when you left your body behind
Like a coat thrown carelessly on the floor,

Did you fly into eternity,
A white bird, by light blinded,

Struggling through icy silence,
Lost to affection?

III

I have no sense any longer of your being anywhere:
The sea is in radiant turmoil beside me,
The sands are a golden stripe along the water's edge,
Whitebreasted tern pipe cacophonous coronachs,
A ship appears from the river, moves briskly onto the ocean :

And nothing offers a counter to the blank naught of your
    absence.

Old Nuns

Their bonnets spread from their faces
Like the wings of white exotic birds;

When they hugged you into their skirts,
You knew how tightly God embraced the world;

Pouches dangled from their waists
With needles, scissors, keys and coloured pens;

Beads rattled when they walked;
Their long pockets held sweets and rainbow balls;

They showed us how letters were made,
Spent patient hours leading tiny fingers along the abacus;

Gloriously they lit our lives.

Sisters

We have chosen to keep
To this small corner of earth,
Watching the same square of sky
In all its changes,
Attending to the slow mutation of tree and flower.

Each day we wake to the familiar bell:
Eating, praying, reading in monotonous sequence,
We turn inward amid the ordinary,
Searching in our hearts
For traces of God.

Red berries on the ash
Remind us that another Summer
Hastens to death.
Still as tissued apples in a box,
We wait by the door for his knock.

Singleness

(for Matthew Hemson on his Ordination)

There will be joy too in your singleness
As when gloom lifts while you listen
From some heart fastened to sorrow,

As when children in schoolyards ambush you
And drag you off to riotous play,
As when affection swamps you in a festive congregation.

As when ailing women you visit in shabby flats
Fall silent
Before the mystery of broken bread,

As when the dying bless you
With their last,
Most precious smiles,

As when, sitting in the silence of automatic prayer,
You know suddenly
You are being visited by God.

The old will shelter in your untidy heart,
The young will know in you
The laughter of Yahweh;

And the wretched see
You have no bride
But them.

Down's Syndrome God

(for Cinnie)

The little boy circles beneath the trees
That circle the field.

Now and again he dashes onto the grass,
Takes sudden fright, runs off to hide again.

The children are busy with football,
Games of run and chase.

He fears their shouting,
He cannot tell whether they will welcome him.

His heart is full of love;
If they but knew their need.

Loveletter

Having no power to lift you from sorrow,
I put my hope in Him who madly loves each living thing,
Who watches fretfully above our billion beds,

Whispering into every weary ear,
Caressing the surfeited and starved,
The whole, the hurt, the brokenhearted;

And when affection swamps my helpless heart,
I trust the pounding seas
Overwhelming Him.

Remembering Paddy : Céide 29.10.97

I

Will anyone think of us in years to come,
Muse on how you blessed our days with kindness,

Driving sorrow, the wolf, from our door,
Building walls against marauding grief,

How you were a star secure in our skies,
Music thrown against silence,

How you were like God himself for us
In your tenderness and your laughter?

II

I feel no anger at your death,
Flailing and floundering though I am
In loss;

More,
An upsurge of gratitude
For the way you blessed us :

We have known the bounty of Autumn
And settle into Winter
With harvest of sweet apples.

Raifteirí

There was never such rain
As when Raifteirí sheltered beneath a scraggy bush
On a forsaken roadside in Connaught.

It seemed like rapeseed thrown at him in hard fistfulls;
It was like a riverburst above him,
Carrying the countryside in its stream.

It gave him an excuse for a poem
And to thank some elseforgotten householder
Who dried him and offered a fragrant bed,
Then woke him to a night of ale and music.

And in the joy of the returned sun,
His heart could bless the bush
And love it for a friend.

De Oude Toren

Van Gogh saw our future:

The Neunen churchtower, derelict in the fields
Surrounded untidily by crosses.

Crows overhead,
A dismal sky.

Even where the sunlight falls,
There is no whisper of hope;

And the flowers
Are blemishes on the grass.

Modern Instances

The balding popstar has installed a tabernacle,
Encrusted with opals,
As a drinks cabinet.

Sanctuary lamps and benediction candelabra
Light public house revelry;
People sit on pews to guzzle booze.

Old altar-tables serve as counters in lingerie boutiques,
Chalices can be had in junkshops
With messages underneath, begging prayers for donors long dead.

In the Cleopatra Gallery,
A monstrance frames a prophylactic in beams of blazing gold,
Ciboria filled with dildos open and close like music boxes.

Was it our presumption on the ineffable that offended you?
We lived, with all our failures, with love and prayer
And gentleness; and pain was pity's welcome burden.

What justice has lured us to this desert,
Our sweet Jerusalem ruined?

The River

"Then he brought me back to the door of the temple: and behold, water was issuing from below the threshold of the temple toward the east" (Ezekiel 47,1)

The river from God's great city,
Carrying life to every desert place,
Gladdening the roots of trees,
Thrilling the hearts of birds,
Runs slurry-grey.

Dead fish float there:
Fish hued as rainbows;
Innocent fish, born to the flow,
Trusting the flow.

Small children sob in the night:
Their faces cloud the dawn.
Images of hardfaced women unsettle our waking,
Of men, cloaking devastation with counterfeit solicitude.

Side by side with them
We built Your Body up,
Channels of living water,
Conduits of unfaltering grace.

We cannot disown them
Now the dream is dead.
Scandalised by ourselves,
We lose faith in You.

The river from God's great city
Runs slurry-grey:
Deadly its flow.

But it is Your face before us
In the broken face of the world,
In the hard faces of our shame,
In the face of each tormented child.

The Agreement: 10.4.1998

Just when we were weary of prayer
And the fruitless drone of our own voices,

When feeling had left our hearts
And we were resigned to a world without wonder,

On a bright Good Friday, Easter dawned;
And we ramble amid the gravecloths singing.

On Hearing Martin Hayes' Barndances
in Glendalough

From all the houses people followed the dance:
Old men we had buried came from their graves,
Age falling away with the clay
As they stretched their limbs in the sun.

Timid ladies stepped daintily out,
Labouring men leapt and huzzahed,
The set-dancers of Glendasan
Trooped down the riverside.

People long-forgotten gathered their bodies up:
Miners and miners' wives,
Bronze age potentates,
Monks and hermits in a long retinue.

Beggarwomen grown proud as queens,
Armies of warworn soldiers,
Companies of nuns,
Kevin himself, surrounded by birds.

Waterhens ran beside us,
Heads thrust out,
Ponies, rabbits, yelping dogs:
The valley of silence was noisy with resurrection.

Easter

A new light shines this Easter morning:
Catkins are rubbed in gold,
Blossoms sparkle on thorn,

Fresh linen covers the altars,
Cars are strung along the roadways outside churches
In chains of dancing colour;

People carry water home to bless the fields,
Mourners move towards graveyards
With glaums of daffodils;

In every home,
Children tear through wraps and ribbons
To reveal the brittle secrets of chocolate eggs;

Amazed,
Even as we shall be amazed
By the secrets of eternity.

Thoughts on Eternity

I

The painted boats move out to sea,
Steered by friends;
They leave without me.

The carousel goes round
With all its horses
But never stops.

People bathe in the river.
The day is warm,
They wave me welcome;

A push and I will plunge,
Panicking, into bliss.

II

We will not notice time
And its heavy passing
Or know it ever was

When we reach the glowing moment
Of eternity.

III

The appletree is burdened by abundance;

The glory of its blossoming past,
It supplicates for hands
To loose its limbs to swoosh to sky again.